A CALL
for
World Peace

A CALL
for
World Peace

AL LIPOLD

A CALL FOR WORLD PEACE

This book is written to provide information and motivation to readers. Its purpose is not to render any type of psychological, legal, or professional advice of any kind. The content is the sole opinion and expression of the author, and not necessarily that of the publisher.

Copyright © 2019 by Al Lipold

All rights reserved. No part of this book may be reproduced, transmitted, or distributed in any form by any means, including, but not limited to, recording, photocopying, or taking screenshots of parts of the book, without prior written permission from the author or the publisher. Brief quotations for noncommercial purposes, such as book reviews, permitted by Fair Use of the U.S. Copyright Law, are allowed without written permissions, as long as such quotations do not cause damage to the book's commercial value. For permissions, write to the publisher, whose address is stated below.

Printed in the United States of America.

ISBN 978-1-64552-121-1   (Paperback)
ISBN 978-1-64552-122-8   (Digital)

Lettra Press books may be ordered through booksellers or by contacting:

Lettra Press LLC
18601 Green Valley Ranch Blvd.
Unit 108, Box 204 Denver, CO 80249
1 303 586 1431 | info@lettrapress.com
www.lettrapress.com

Contents

Introduction vii

Acceptance of Who We Are 1
Rights of Every Person This Includes All Women 3
Love, Peace, and the Future Era 7
Bits of This and That about Current Affairs 11
Hope for Individuals and Humanity 15
Albert Einstein and Elie Wiesel 17
Terrorism and Extremism 1 21
Terrorism and Extremism 2 23
Terrorism and Extremism 3 25
Terrorism and Extremism 4 29
The Third World 33
Hopefully Peace 35
World Peace 39
About the Author 43

Introduction

Over the past few years and from time to time, I have made written notes of matters that relate to war and peace, justice, hatred and oppression, politics, race relations, and more recently, terrorism and extremism. This information I mostly collected from news items in newspapers, magazines, and books that I read.

I have focused on who we are, as individuals and groups, are. The rights of every person, hatred, free will, hope, faith, love and peace, and of course, terrorism and extremism.

My ultimate focus has been on peace on this earth. Is world peace possible? I am of the opinion, yes, world peace is possible.

Some of the world characters that I read about, and admired, as I considered my quest for information and understanding were Winston Churchill, Albert Einstein, Elie Wiesel, and Pope John Paul II and our current pope, Francis I.

This book is written to cover and link together some of the above referred-to matters. And as far as the United States is concerned, one of the first notes I made referred to then President Woodrow Wilson, who on April 16,1917, asked congress to declare a war to end all wars.

We were on the winning side in the World War I, but it did not end all wars. However, by the end of the war, the United States had become a first-class military power.

Acceptance of Who We Are

Who am I? Who are you? Who are they? I like to refer to Popeye the Sailorman.

He was a fictional character who, over the years, appeared in comic strips, theatre, and television and animated cartoons. One of his favorite sayings was "I am Popeye the Sailorman, I am who I am, and that is all that I am, I'm Popeye the Sailorman."

No one had a choice in becoming who he or she is, black, white, yellow, male, or female. Each one of us is who he or she is, and that is all that we are, just like Popeye the Sailorman.

Each human being is different from all others. We do however, have a common humanity. It has been written (among other places) in the US Declaration of Independence that God made all human beings equal. It says in the Bible (Genesis 1:26-27) that all men and women are made in God's image.

Modern genetics has demonstrated conclusively that no such thing as race exists. Thanks to the mapping of the human genome, we now know that each person shares 99.99 percent of his or her genetic material with everyone else. Similarly, skin color and physiognomy are now no longer regarded as the most obvious ways of classifying people by the scientific community (Suicide of a Super Power, p. 135). Admittedly, though, try as one might, he or she cannot be Albert Einstein, Marie Curie, Enrico Caruso, Maria

Callas, Babe Ruth, or Serena Williams. We are who we are, and that is all that we are.

To paraphrase St. Paul, there is neither Jew nor Arab, slave nor free, male nor female, black nor white. We are all one in God. That is, we share the gift of life and a common humanity. We are equal children of God. We must pray, listen, learn, think, and act in such a way that all people everywhere will know that we truly believe that black lives matter because all lives matter.

We can and should treat others with the decency and courtesy that each man, woman, and child deserves merely by virtue of their humanity. Only when we regard others as individuals and act toward them, with kindness, justice, and mercy and compassion do we move beyond labels (America 4-27-15, p. 6).

Life has no option but to carry on; it must always play the best hand it can no matter how poor and disastrous the hand might be, and no matter who or what offers the challenge (Life's Solution, Morris, p. 12).

Every life counts and is meaningful. The rights of every person, man, woman and child, is worthy of respect, dignity, and individual freedom. These rights should not be denied to any of them by any government, political, religious, military, or other organization or group. Thomas Paine wrote that all people are "equal in the order of creation" (Common Sense, p. XVI).

Rights of Every Person
This Includes All Women

If the world is to survive, then all lives matter. The day must come when the law will not tell the difference between a man and a woman, a black person and a white person, an Asian or an Indian, rich or poor. All human beings should be able to realize their full potential. Women and men should have the same opportunities to influence developments at all levels of society. God intended that the earth and everything in it be for the use of all human beings.

> "How many women have been and still are valued more for their physical appearance than for their personal qualities, professional competence, intellectual work, the richness of their sensitivity and, finally for the very dignity of their being. And what can be said then for the obstacles that in so many parts of the world still prevent women from being fully involved in social, political and economic life?" (Genesis. Lesson 17, CSSI)

Shouldn't women obtain the same opportunities as men to influence developments at all levels of society, It has been claimed that the biological differences between men and women are minor compared with their overwhelming anatomical correspondences and the natural complementarity of the sexes and the fact humankind could not exist without both argues for a moral equality that should rightly inform social consideration, then men and women will cease to be two absolutely different and antagonistic identities, and each will be able to realize their full potential in the greater whole of human kind (The Undivided Past, p. 135).

Aristotle once said the issue was not the balancing of individual rights and responsibilities, as we would put it today, but the fact that we live our lives not only as Individuals but also as members of society.

Recently, and as a sign of the future, a petition signed by almost fifteen thousand women in Saudi Arabia calling for an end to male guardianship was sent to the government under Saudi law. At present, women need the consent of a male guardian, usually a family member for major decisions like travel or health care (Time, Oct. 10, 2016). The Muslim world, in particular, sooner or later must realize that this is not now the eighth or ninth century. Muslim men must come to realize that if it were not for women, there would be no men. Also that they, the men, had no choice in being a man or woman at birth.

Hirsi Ali, author of the books Heretic and Nomad, expresses outrage that Muslim women are treated as second-class citizens. Men take up to four wives. Ali says, while women are limited to one husband. Further at least five thousand women are put to death in so-called honor killings each year. The author cites the case of a twenty-four-year-old Pakistani woman who married against her father's wishes and was stoned to death outside a courthouse. Hillary Clinton said that, "Human rights are women's rights. Let us not forget that among those rights are the right to speak freely, and the right to be heard." She also said that there cannot be true democracy unless women's voices are heard "and that there cannot be true democracy unless all citizens are able to participate in the lives of their country." It has been said that the "clash of civilizations" between the Islamic world and the West has been caused, in part, by the poor treatment of Muslim women. This paper suggests that women in the Middle's East are underrepresented in the workforce and in government because of oil, not Islam . . . The failure of women to join the non-agricultural labor force has profound social consequences: It leads to higher fertility rates, less education for girls, and less female influence with the family. Is also has far reaching political consequences; when fewer women work outside the home, they are less likely to exchange information and overcome collective action problems, less likely to mobilize politically and to lobby for expanded rights, and less likely to gain representation in government. This leaves oil-producing states with atypically strong patriarchal cultures and political institutions (Thomas L. Friedman, Hot, Flat, and Crowded, p. 102).

The Muslims must overcome the oppression of women and the lack of free and individual choice (Nomad XII).

Love, Peace, and the Future Era

"We should respect the foreigner and immigrant people of different cultures and worthy of being listened to. We must arm our children with the weapons of dialogue, we must find some way . . . to gain eternal peace for the world." (Eisenhower, A Soldier's Life, p. 705)

On August 6, 1945, an American B29 bomber dropped the first atomic bomb over Hiroshima, Japan, and approximately eighty thousand people were killed and thirty-five thousand wounded. On August 15 and after the second atomic bomb was dropped over Nagasaki, Japan announced its surrender. At the end of World War II, Albert Einstein said we won the war but not the peace. Our current pope, Francis I, stated that the way to peace is to give nonviolence a chance.

Every person, hopefully, should grow physically and spiritually capable of making courageous choices and decisions, in order to build daily, even though little things, a world peace. We must make a commitment to justice, to the dignity of each human life, and to the truth that all human rights begin when human lives begin and not any moment later.

Bishop John Noonan wrote in part, we need "a deep desire to change the world, to transmit values, to leave this world somehow better than when we found it with all its tragedies, its hopes and aspirations, its strength and weaknesses. The earth is our common home and all of us are brothers and sisters. God desires that we help to build a civilizations of love, one in which all human beings have freedom and opportunity to experience the love of God and live out that love by making a free gift of themselves to one another. Further, we are a nation of immigrants, struggling to address the challenges of many new immigrants in our midst. We are a powerful nation, confronting terror and trying to build a safer, more just, more powerful world. We are concerned about the dignity of the human person, about the sacredness of every human life, because we are of God" (The Florida Catholic, August 26, 2016).

We cannot change history. However, we can learn from it. We can study it. Reflect and discuss on it and, most of all, learn from it. The day may dawn when fair play, love for our fellow man, and respect for justice and freedom will enable tormented generations to march forth serene and triumphant from the hideous epoch in which we have to dwell.

Fifty years ago, Pope John XIII, shortly before his death and the assassination of President Kennedy, left a testament to the world that is still relevant today. In his encyclical on peace and human rights, *Pacem in Terris*, the pope, wrote that true and lasting peace among nations must consist of mutual trust. This trust is important among allies and essential among adversaries. Relationships among nations cannot be driven by fear, competition and excessive reliance upon espionage. There must be a level of trust that allows for greater collaboration in facing the global challenges and security needs that affect us all (America, Nov.18, 2013).

Pope Francis's challenge to us is to return to the Gospel and embrace nonviolence as the way to be peacemakers. Nelson Mandela's life story illustrates the possibility of this conversion. He said the logic of violence has had its reign long enough. Can we too give nonviolence a chance? (America, Jan. 20, 2014).

Peace, said the pope, must be built on justice, socioeconomic development, freedom, respect for fundamental human rights, the participation of all in public affairs, and the building of trust between peoples (America, Dec. 2014). The whole international community has to step up to find a long-term solution for peace throughout the world. He said, "It is love which must inspire humanity today, if it is to face the crisis of the meaning of life ... and especially the duty to defend the dignity of every human person. Each person is precious in the eyes of God. Christ gave his life for each one of us" (Pope John Paul II).

Socrates stated, "One word frees us of all the weight and pain in life. That word is love."

"Love is the only force capable of transforming an enemy into a friend" (Martin Luther King Jr).

You learn to speak by speaking, to study by studying, to work by working, and, just so you learn to love by loving. All those who think to learn in any other way deceives them. St. Francis de Sales

No one is born hating others because of the color of his skin, or their background, or their religion. People learn to hate, and if they can learn to hate, they can be taught to love, for love comes more naturally to the human heart than its opposite" (Nelson Mandela).

In Nixon's first inaugural address, in January 1969, he said, "No man can be fully free while his neighbour is not. To go forward at all is to go forward together, as one nation, not two. The laws have caught up with our conscience. What remains to give life to what is in the law: to ensure at last that all are born equal in dignity before God, all are born equally in dignity before man."

Can we, in the twenty-first century, give to the world that peace which has up to now been forthcoming? That is, a peace that is based on truth, justice, love, and freedom for all?

It would be great if we could reach the conclusion that our children should not be robbed of their inheritance or denied of their right to live in a free and peaceful world.

Bits of This and That about Current Affairs

All over the world there exists poverty, hatred, and oppression. How do we overcome this? The great mass of current refugees in the world shows that there is a great need for reconciliation, peace, love, and forgiveness.

Pope Francis said that we must regain the conviction that we need one another and that we have a shared responsibility for others in this world. He stated that violence of man against man is a contradiction to every religion that merits the name. The pope has said, referring to Christianity, Judaism and Islam: "Every human being is a creature of God, is our brother regardless of his origin or religious beliefs."

Should we, as former President John F. Kennedy said, "If we cannot now end our diversities at least we can make the world safe for diversity." It has been said that man's aggressive behavior is ingrained in us. Let us hope that this behavior does not lead to our extinction.

Pope John XIII wrote that there are problems of universal dimensions that cannot be adequately addressed except by a structure of the same proportions that can act in an effective manner on a worldwide basis. The moral order therefore demands that such a form of public authority be established.

There seems to be a tendency, without reason, to make sweeping generalizations of people, by gender, by religion, by culture, and by race. For example, some people hate people because of their religion. They know very little if anything about the religion and yet they make sweeping generalizations that are deep set and extremely hard to overcome. They hate black people just because they are black. They hate Jews just because they are Jews.

"Every day we allow someone to talk us into negotiating rather than annihilating, they draw one step closer. People that have never met you, that have never even seen you, hate you with every fibre of their being. They hate you because you're free. They hate you because you represent to them everything they want but can never have because they are slaves to an oppressive and consuming philosophy of hatred that drives them to the point of a yearning desire to die taking your freedom rather than winning their own . . . They feed on the hatred of America and all she stands for. Remember, if their hatred is stronger than your resolve, they win." (Paul Valentine, *The Conservative Handbook*, p. 184)

Martin Luther King reportedly said, "Darkness cannot drive out darkness, only light can do that, Hate cannot drive out hate, only love can do that." We must always keep in mind the dignity of every human being. We must be concerned with the national, racial, ethnic, economic, and ideological background of every person. As we move forward into the third decade of the twenty-first century, the pace of society continues to move at an accelerating pace.

"Each of us must rededicate ourselves to serving the common good. We are a community. Our individual's fates are linked; our futures intertwined; and we act in the knowledge and in that spirit together, as the Bible says: We can move mountains." (Jimmy Carter)

We must work together to overcome poverty. We must join together with others around the world to pursue peace and protect human rights and religious liberty.

Dostoevsky wrote "that if God does not exist, then everything is permitted." Then there is a tendency to act as gods with nothing to restrain them.

Jesse Owens, famous athlete, said that battles that count aren't for medals. The struggles are within yourself. That's where it is at. He won four gold medals in track during 1936 Olympics in Berlin.

Pope Francis, speaking to many of the world's most prominent corporate and nonprofit leaders, said, "Tens of millions of people, a huge share of them children have been left stateless by war and poverty. Too many people have little or no access to systems that have brought prosperity to the developed world." Then he offered what may be the great challenge to corporate titans gathered, "I pray too that you may involve in your efforts those whom you seek to help; give them a voice, listen to their stories, learn from their experiences, and understand their needs. See in them a brother and a sister, a son and a daughter, a mother and a father. Amid the challenges of our day, see the human face of those you earnestly seek to help" (Fortune, Jan.2017, pp. 9 and 11).

Hope for Individuals and Humanity

"Hope is an optimistic attitude of mind that is based on expectations of positive outcomes related to events and circumstances in one's life or in the world at large. Hope is linked to the existence of a goal, combined with a determined plan for reaching that goal." (Wikipedia)

The impact that hope can have on aspects of life such as health, work, education, and personal meaning. Hope has the ability to help people heal. Individuals, who maintain hope, especially when battling illness, significantly enhance their chance of recovery. Hope is viewed as a motivational and cognitive attribute that is theoretically necessary to initiate and sustain action to goal attainment.

In theology and from ancient times, people have recognized that a spirit of hope had the power to heal afflictions and help them bear times of great suffering, illnesses, disaster, loss, and pain caused by the malevolent spirits and events.

Today, we are at the brink unprecedented global destruction, global warming, and global violence.

We are agents of transformation who cooperate with God to transfigure his world. Remember the story of God's conversation with Moses "I have seen the suffering of my people." Our God is a God who knows and sees and hears; there is hope that nightmares will end, hope that seemingly intractable problems will find solutions. God has some tremendous partners. Christian hope is fundamentally based on love of God for everyone: rich and poor, black and white, gay and straight, Jew and Arab, Palestinian and Israeli, Serb and Albanian, Hutu and Tutsi, Pakistani and Indian, none are outside the purview of God's love.

Remember what Jesus said? "I, if I am lifted up, will draw all to me." Not some but all (America, Apr. 14, 2016).

As human beings, we have made tremendous advances in arts, literature, science, and economics, but have lagged behind in human relations. We hope that everyone should be treated equally, that is, no one should be treated as being inferior. As individuals, we had no choice in becoming who we are.

"God is coming to judge the earth. He will judge the world with righteousness, and the people with equity. The coming judgement is a promise of hope for humanity to turn to righteousness, to walk away from evil. The work of the church is to act in ordinary ways that create hope and not despair over devil." (America, 11-7-16)

Christian believers who have read to the end of the Bible have the confidence that no matter how challenging things can be, the ultimate outlook will be positive and victorious. That is one reason, among many, that there should be no gloom and doom; in the mind, heart or, spirit of a true believer (Mike Huckabee, p. 197). In short, all is not lost. God's love prevails.

Albert Einstein and Elie Wiesel

Two books I read recently, one about Albert Einstein, the other about Elie Wiesel, impressed me with their thinking regarding current affairs and the future of this world.

Albert Einstein

He was born in 1879 and died in 1956. He was a German-born theoretical physicist who developed the general theory of relativity, among other feats. He was one of the most recognized and well-known scientists of the century. *Time* magazine portrayed him as the greatest mind of the century. He was also known as a great humanist.

The following are quotations from the book *How to Think Like Einstein* by Daniel Smith:

In 1918, as he put it to his friend Heinrich Zanger. "The mainspring of scientific thought is not an external goal toward which one must strive, but the pleasure of thinking." There should be a better and genuine understanding among nations to lessen the likelihood of another dreadful catastrophe (p. 144). Racial prejudice can be remedied by enlightenment and education. It is a slow and painstaking process in which all people should take part (p. 145).

"I am a human being, and only a human being without any special attachment to any state or national entity whatever" (p 147).

"The psychological roots of war are biologically rooted in the aggressive nature of the male creature" (p. 157). "Every country will have to surrender a portion of its sovereignty through international cooperation to avoid destruction, aggression must be sacrificed" (p. 158). "Civil liberty, tolerance and equality of all citizens before the law prevail" (p. 159). "As the old aphorism had it, evil prevails when men do nothing. Everyone should be respected as a citizen, individual but no one idolized (p. 173). There is a whole lot of work we need to do in the world, starting with ourselves and our families. He also said that the world is a dangerous place, not because of those who do evil, but because of those who look on and do nothing.

Elie Wiesel

He was born in 1928 and died in 2016. He was a Romanian-born America-Jewish writer, professor, and political activist. He was Holocaust survivor and author who fought for peace, human rights, and human decency. He became a global activist and orator. He won the Nobel Peace Prize in 1986. He wrote fifty-seven books, internationally acclaimed works of fiction and nonfiction.

The following are quotations from the book *Night* by Elie Wiesel:

Upon receiving the Nobel Peace Prize, he said, "Thank you (to those in attendance) for helping human kind make peace it's most urgent and noble aspiration. I have tried to keep memory alive, that I have tried to fight those who would forget. We are guilty, we are accomplices. I swore never to be silent whenever and wherever human beings endure suffering and humiliation. We must take sides. Neutrality helps the oppressor, never the victim. Silence encourages the tormentor, never the tormented. Wherever men and women are persecuted because of their race, religion, or political views, that place must, at that moment, becomes the center of the universe. There is so much injustice and suffering crying out for our attention: victims of hunger, of racism, and political persecution. Human suffering anywhere concerns men and women everywhere. Violence is not the answer. Terrorism is the most dangerous of answers. The refugees and their misery, the children and their fears, the uprooted and their hopelessness. Something must be done about their situation. But I have faith. Faith in the God of Abraham, Isaac and Jacob, and even in his creation. Without it no action would be possible. We must seek to achieve a peace that is based on truth, justice, love and freedom for all."

He also said that wherever men and women are persecuted because of their race, religion, or personal views, that place at that moment must become the center of the universe.

Terrorism and Extremism 1

Terrorism is the unlawful use of force and violence against persons or property to intimidate or coerce a government, the civilian population, or any segment thereof, in furtherance of political or social objectives.

Extremism means a tendency or disposition to go to extremes, especially in political matters. For example, Nazi extremism, fear from what most people consider correct or reasonable. Today, extremism is an ideology of savagery, videotapes of beheadings and burnings of human beings as propaganda tools for terrorism.

Terrorism and extremism must be eliminated if the world is to enjoy a period of peace. Right at the beginning, unanswered questions should be raised. What is going to happen next? Can we overcome and defeat terrorism and extremism as it now exists in the world?

Terrorism is not a religious act. Every religion, including Islam, considers the killing of human beings to be a violation of the very principles of religion. The Quran specifically forbids aggressive warfare and permits war only in self-defense. Later Islamic, or Sharia law that is based on the Sunnah, or habits and practices of the Prophet Muhammad, forbids Muslims to attack a country were Muslims are permitted to practice their faith freely; the killing of civilians is prohibited, as is the destruction of property and the use of fire in warfare. Muslims around the world have and continue to disown terrorism, but this is rarely reported by the Western media. Terrorism is simply a political act, which uses tha language of religion to rationalize irreligious political acts (Robt Kess, 6-11-09).

Historically, wars were fought tribe against tribe, nation against nation, man against man, soldier against soldier. Today, war has changed to the degree that the enemy is anyone whom the terrorists and extremists deem to be the opponent. That is, old men, women, children, religious or nonreligious groups of people. The so-called soldier might be a child, wrapped up with explosives. The target could be anyone such as women, children, old men, and people of any religious sect. They do not care who they kill or how many, even of their own religion, to gain their objective. Their war is not one of religion but of politics.

It is interesting to note that Koran demanded constant revision and self-examination. All rightly faith comes from God (Muhammad, p. 395, *A History of God*, Karen Armstrong).

It is also interesting to note that suicide is forbidden in Islamic ethics and is considered to be a major sin. It is said that God is the only one who has the right to end the life of a person. Does this not include the suicide bombers?

It is the opinion or many that terrorism and extremism will not just go away. They will have to be put away by force or show of force.

Terrorism and Extremism 2

Who are the terrorists and extremists? Islam in and of itself is not one of them. However, there are some Muslims who use their faith to promote their own political gains. Their primary goal is not to promote Islam but rather to achieve political gain and dominance. Many Muslims are now living in a society that has not kept up with time. It is now the twenty-first century and not the eighth or ninth century. It is time for them, in a sense, to wake up.

Within the past few years, we have seen an increase in terrorism and extremism in different parts of the world. Now we are experiencing a tremendous movement of people leaving their country to another either welcomed or unwelcomed. What does the year 2017 and beyond hold in relation to a peaceful settlement of these people?

The indiscriminant killing of human beings, by suicide bombers, etc., cannot be justified under any circumstances. This in particular where the victims are not combatants, associated or not associated with the enemy. Every individual has a right to a life, whatever that life may consist of, and wherever on earth where it exists.

The following are quotations from the book *The ISIS Apocalypse* by William McCants:

"Leading the Muslim community into a battle for which it is not ready, a battle that will be revolting and in which blood will be spilled... so be it. This is exactly what ISIS wants, since right and wrong no longer have any place in the current situation" (p. 17). Islam was born into a tribal society that lacked formal laws in a state to enforce them. Each tribe abided by its own customs and cult. The founder of Islam, Muhammad, was able to create a state because he appealed to a greater religious identity to unite the fractious tribes. Doing that required him to promulgate laws that could transcend tribal identity and regulate a state. As a consequence, Islam's scriptures cover everything from inheritance to warfare. (Judaism emerged in a similar environment, which accounts for some of the parallels between the two religions.) Although some of Muhammad's legislation is harsh by modern standards, jihadist view it as a readymade kit for enforcing rule in tribal societies. And Muhammad's life provides a model for how to do it successfully (p. 56-57).

"One of the most important goals and their most prominent duty must be an effort to establish an economic power" (p. 67). "But we consider this the final goal, that will result in the final goal and bringing about the downfall of the greatest power. America" (p. 88).

The Islamic State requires power, authority, and control of territory (p. 116). The Islamic State believes in a prophecy which requires the conquest of every country on earth (p. 139). The point is that the extreme brutality is not incompatible with establishing a new state, it may not be wisest course of action, and it probably won't create a state that many people would want to live in. But that doesn't mean it won't work. Just as most people can't imagine the brutality would be a winning political strategy. They also can't imagine that any religious scripture would justify such a thing. Muslims and non-Muslims are equally baffled as to how anyone would commit atrocities in the name of God (p. 150).

The Islamic State believes it is better to be feared than to be loved and deliberately strokes the anger of international onlookers, but the group also tried to provide government services to its subjects. But there's another way to reconcile the contradictions: The group is devoted to establishing an ultraconservative Islamic state at all costs, so it modifies its religious and political doctrines when they get in the way of that goal.

Terrorism and Extremism 3

Today, people are on the move in unprecedented numbers. Some move voluntarily drawn by economic opportunities or family ties. Some sixty-five million and growing have been forcibly uprooted by war, persecution, ethnic and religious strife, dire poverty, natural catastrophe, or environmental degradation. Their number is equivalent to the entire population of Great Britain (America, 2017).

Mikhail Gorbachev, former leader of Soviet Union and author of *The New Russia*, stated that the dialogue should focus on fighting terrorism. This is indeed an important, urgent task. But as a core of a normal relationship and eventual partnership, it is not enough. The focus should once again be on preventing war, phasing out the arms race and reducing arsenals. The goal should be to agree not just on nuclear weapons' levels and ceilings but also on missile defence and strategic stability. In the modern world, wars must be outlawed, because none of the global problems we are facing can be resolved by war, not poverty, the environment, migration, population growth, or shortage of resource (*Time*, Feb. 13, 2017).

Pope Francis, in his New Year's greetings, declared that 2017 will be good to the degree that people do good and reject hatred as he prayed for those courageously dealing with terrorism gripping the world in "fear and bewilderment." The New Year will be good to the measure in each of us, with the help of God, tries to do good day by day, that's how peace is created. Francis told a crowd of fifty thousand gathered in St. Peter's Square, our leaders must find the resolve and courage to speak out against strength built on immoral foundations. We could have a positive impact if we are persistent.

The Chaldean Catholic patriarch, Louis Sako of Bagdad, called for a united and strong stance, by Muslims and non-Muslims alike, to stop the spread of the cancer of the Islamic State and other terrorists groups. In a statement released on August 27, the patriarch said it is time for Muslims and non-Muslim people of goodwill around the world to deal seriously with situation, especially when we know that the majority of the Muslims are neutral, unbiased, open-minded, and willing to work hard for the benefit of their countries and their fellow citizens. The patriarch called for Muslims to show the real face of Islam and confirm that extremism is contrary to their beliefs. The patriarch said that Christians are waiting for governments and religious authorities to work together to confront and dismantle terrorism and extremism. Steps to achieve this goal include reforms in the curricula in schools, which he said are the major source for teaching extremism.

Islam, in my opinion, should be a society whose aim should be the salvation of its adherents and not the conquest of the world. Again, Pope Francis said there is an urgent need for all religions to work together for peace, through dialogue, and to reject the use of God's name to justify violence (America, 9-26-16, p. 25). Christianity had its holy wars, too, but then it had its reformation. Now Islam must have its reformation. Islam needs a Nelson Mandela or Mahatma Gandhi to bring Islam into the twenty-first century. They must divorce themselves from terrorism and extremism in any form.

In God, hope triumphs over despair, love triumphs over hate, two pillars of eternal truth. We should never separate ourselves from others simply because of their race, nationality, occupation, politics, educational background, or social status.

Migrants and migration have bedeviled every European leader since a refugee crisis exploded in 2015. That year, a record 1.3 million people from the Middle East, Africa, and Asia applied for Asylum in Europe, seeking refuge from violence, poverty, oppression. Most notable from Syria (America, 9-20-16). These conflicts are causing a refugee crisis of a dimension not seen since World War II, involving some 60 million people (America, 9-26-16).

Perhaps Winston Churchill had the answer. He stated that civilization will not last, freedom will not survive, peace will not be kept, unless a large majority of mankind unite together to defend them and show themselves possessed of a constabulary power (a police force organized like the military) before which barbaric and atavistic forces will stand in awe (Civilization).

This means the free world, and I mean world. They must unite together with one objective, and that is to defeat for once and all time, the terrorists and extremists all over the world. Only in this way can we give nonviolence a chance. Would it not be great if the free nations of the world, the United States, Russia, China, all of free Europe, Latin America, Africa, India, etc., all got together for this purpose?

Terrorism and Extremism 4

That makes America a very different target indeed for the biggest challenge since Soviet Communism to confront the western world: the threat of radical Islam *(Nomad, p. 125, Ayaan Hirsi Ali)*.

Dick Cheney served as the forty-sixth vice president of the United States (2001-2009). On the day after 9/11, he stated "The first war of the twenty-first century wouldn't simply be a conflict of nation against nation, army against army. It would be first and foremost a war against terrorist who operated in the shadows, feared no deterrent, and would use any weapon they could get their hands on to destroy us" (*In My Time*, Dick Cheney, p. 10).

So long as people do not care to exercise their freedom, those who wish to tyrannize will do so; for tyrants are active and ardent, and will devote themselves in the name of any number of gods, religions and otherwise, to put shackles upon sleeping men (Voltaire, p. 36). In April 2017, United States President Donald Trump ordered the bombing of a Syrian military airport. This because of the Syrian government's use of chemical weapons against citizens. During his campaign for the presidency of the United States, Donald Trump said our goal is not to spread democracy but rather to defeat ISIS and to destroy terrorist organizations.

A pair of bomb attacks at churches in Egypt killed at least forty-four people on April 9 (2017), Shattering the Christian festival of Palm Sunday for the country Copts, the Middle East's largest

Christian community. One bomb ripped through a church in the Nile Delta town of Tanta while a suicide bomber set off his device at an Alexandria cathedral where Coptic Pope Tawadros II had held Palm Sunday services. The attacks were quickly claimed by the Islamic State which has become a persistent menace in Egypt since an insurgent menace in the Sinai Peninsula proclaimed its allegiance in 2014.

In keeping with ISIS sectarian absolutism, the Sinai militants, who in recent years had killed more than a thousand soldiers and police, soon expanded their targets to include Egypt's Christian community, which makes up about 10 percent of the populations (*Time*, April 14, 2017). When terrorist organizations use their own followers as weapons to be launched against defenseless and unsuspecting people, they clearly show the death wish that feeds them. Terrorism springs from hatred, and it generates isolation, mistrust, and closure. Violence is added to violence in a tragic sequence that exasperates successive generations, each one inheriting the hatred which divided those that went before. Terrorism is built on contempt for human life (John Paul, *The Great Mercy Pope*, p. 251). Those who kill by acts of terrorism actually despair of humanity, of life, of the future. In their view, everything is to be hated and destroyed. Terrorists hold that the truth in which they believe or the suffering that they have undergone is so absolute that their reaction in destroying even innocent lives is justified. Terrorism is often the outcome of that fanatic fundamentalism which springs from the conviction that one's own vision of the truth must be forced upon everyone else (John Paul, *The Great Mercy Pope*, p. 252). In this whole effort, religious leaders have a weighty responsibility. The various Christian confessions as well as the world's great religions need to work together to eliminate the social and cultural causes of terrorism. They can do this by teaching the greatness and dignity of the human person and by spreading a clearer sense of the oneness of the human family. This is a specific area of ecumenical and interreligious dialogue and cooperation, a pressing service which religion can offer to world peace.

In undertaking such a commitment, the various religions cannot but pursue the path of that religions can give to peace and against terrorism consists precisely in their teaching forgiveness, for those who forgive and seek forgiveness knows that there is a higher truth, and that by accepting that truth they can transcend themselves (John Paul, *The Great Mercy Pope,* p. 256).

Pope John Paul II writes: "Terrorism," he says, "is often the outcome of that fanatic fundamentalism which springs from the conviction that one's own vision of the truth must be forced upon everyone else." Terrorism exploits both people and God; the Pope says, "It ends by making God and idol to be used for one's own purposes." The Pope believes "terrorism is built on contempt for human life. For this reason, not only does it commit intolerable crimes, because it resorts to terror as a political and military means it is itself a true crime against humanity" (John Paul, *The Great Mercy Pope*).

The Third World

The third world is the aggregate of the underdeveloped nations in the world, especially in Africa or Asia, or made up of minority groups within larger predominant cultures.

In addition to terrorism and extremism, the third world now faces many other pressing problems such as widespread poverty and inequality as set forth in the book, *The World* on *Fire*, dated in 2003, by Amy Chua.

The Following is quoted from the cover of Amy Chua's book: "After the fall of the Berlin Wall, a consensus emerged, not only in the West but elsewhere-that the magical combination of free markets and democracy would transform the world into a community of modernized, peace-loving nations, and individuals into civic minded citizens and consumers. Ethnic hatred, religious zealotry, and other backward aspects of underdevelopment would be swept away."

This did not happen. However, we know "in the developing world today the poor are far more numerous, poverty is more extreme, and inequality far more glaring than in the Western countries, either today or at analogous historical periods. The ongoing population explosion outside the West only make things worse. If the current World Bank projections are correct, the population in countries now classified as developing is expected to increase from roughly four billion today to roughly eight billion by the year 2050. Meanwhile the countries of the world lack the West's well established rule of law traditions. As a result, political transitions in the developing countries tend to be marked not by continuity, but rather by abrupt upheavals, military intervention, violence and bloodshed" (*World on Fire, p. 179*).

Today, an ordinary citizen of a poor undemocratic Muslim country or a civil servant in a third world country or in a former socialist republic struggling to make ends meet is aware of how insubstantial is his share of the world's wealth; he knows that he lives under conditions that are much harsher and more devastating than those of a "Westerner and that he is condemned to a much shorter life. At the same time, however, he senses in a corner of his mind that property is to some considerable degree the fault of his own folly and inadequacy, or those of his father and grandfather. The Western world is scarcely aware of this overwhelming feeling of humiliation that is experienced by most of the world's population" (Turkish writer Orhan Pamuk, p. 258, *World on Fire*).

Ten of the poorest nations of the world are Togo, Madagascar, Afghanistan, Guinea, Mozambique, Ethiopia, Mali, Guinea-Biszau, Comoros, and Haiti. These are countries of the third world. Just recently, in May of 2017, it was announced that in Yemen, 60 percent of its population was in dire poverty. So add Yemen to the list.

Like other group hatred movements directed against market-dominant minorities, Islamic fundamentalism offers an alternative to humiliation. It offers a scapegoat, a mission, an identity, and a chance, however deluded, for the powerless to gain power (*World on Fire, p. 258*).

Hopefully Peace

As we move forward into the third decade of the twenty-first century, the pace of society continues to move at an accelerating pace. It has been said that "visions of economic cooperation are a mirage in the absence of political leaders with the courage to make pace . . . for the sake of all of us . . . we must pray that we can overcome the hatreds and suspicions that have kept us so long divided" (*Our Last Best Chance*, King Abdulla II of Jordan, p. 74).

Sun Tzu said 2,500 years ago, "Winning 100 battles is not the acme of skill, to subdue the enemy without fighting is the acme of skill" (Ronald Reagan, *The Notes*, p. 69). Dwight Eisenhower stated that "The vital element on keeping peace is our military establishment. Our arms must be mighty, ready for instant action, so that no potential aggressor may be tempted to risk its own destruction" (Ronald Reagan, *The Notes*, p. 70). "It is interesting to note that as of the year 2011 we have sent over 43 million Americans to war of some kind in our nation's 232 years of history: 1.2 million of them gave their lives for the rest of us" (Huckabee, p. 206).

Not long ago, observers might have thought that tensions across the Berlin Wall or between the factions of Northern Ireland would never be eased, and yet those struggles are now mostly memories. Why not aim to do the same in the Middle East (*Our Last Best Chance*).

Lasting peace in the Middle East seems to have grown ever more remote. It may be that peace is a process, not a destination. And try as we might to imagine otherwise, we are stuck with each other, in all our current state of humanity. So why not break bread and talk it out? (July 10, 2017, America).

United States President Nixon talked about the need for peace between the Israelis and Arabs and said, "It takes courage, a different kind of courage to wage peace . . . continuous war in this area is not a solution to Israel's survival and above all, it is not right" (*Inner Circles, Alexander Haig Jr., pp. 462-3*).

"As between Israel and Palestine, both sides have a moral responsibility to strive for peace. They also have very compelling pragmatic imperative to do so: the alternative is more conflict and violence" (*Our Last Best Chance*)

In regards to the need for peace between the Israelis and Arabs, United States President Nixon said, "It takes courage, a different kind of courage, to wage peace. Continuous war in this area is not a solution to Israel's survival and, above all. It is not right." He also said, "What a lot of people understand, is you don't quit" (Haig, *Inner Circles,* p. 462).

Martin Luther King Jr., said, "We must learn to live together as brothers or perish together as fools." John F. Kennedy said, "Mankind must put an end to war or war will put an end to mankind" (Ronald Reagan, *The Notes,* pp. 57, 59).

As long as nations cannot learn to live cooperatively, there will be conflict or war, and as long as there are aggressors, there will be resisters.

If and when the world does defeat ISIS and other terrorist and extremist organizations, then perhaps the world could enjoy a period of peace.

The world now must contend with nuclear, chemical, and biological weapons that can wipe out large segments of our populations in mere moments (Valentine, *The Conservative Handbook,* p. 117).

"In every continent, from the depth of human suffering, a cry for mercy seems to rise to up. Where hatred and the thirst for revenge dominate, where war brings suffering and death to the innocent, there the grace of mercy is needed in order to settle human minds and hearts and to bring about peace. Wherever respect for life and human dignity are lacking, there is need of God's merciful love, in whose light we see the inexpressible value of every human being. Mercy is needed on order to ensure that every injustice in the world will come to an end in the splendour for truth" (John Paul II, *The Great Mercy Pope*, p. 263).

"Injustices in the world can never be used to excuse acts of terrorism. The Pope urges world religions to work together to eliminate the social and cultural cause of terrorism, and to take the lead in publicity condemning terrorism and denying terrorists any form of moral legitimacy. He adds that the help that religions can give to peace and against terrorism consists precisely in their teaching forgiveness. Forgiveness is the opposite of resentment and revenge, not of justice" (John Paul II, *The Great Mercy Pope*, p. 122).

World Peace

"World Peace, or peace on earth, is an ideal state of freedom, peace, and happiness among and within all nations and people. This ideal of world non-violence provides a basis for peoples and nations to willingly cooperate either voluntarily or by virtue of a system of governance that prevents warfare. For example, since 1945, the United Nations and the five permanent members of its Security Council (the United States, Russia, China, France and the UK) have worked to resolve conflicts without war. However, nations have entered numerous military conflicts since that time." (Wikipedia)

Former United States President Jimmy Carter is alleged to have said, "Despite theological differences, all religions share common commitments . . . I am convinced that Christians, Buddhist, Jews and others can embrace each other in a common effort to alleviate human suffering and to espouse peace" (Kelly-Gangi, *The Essential Wisdom of the World's Greatest Thinkers, p. 93*). He also said, "Each of us must rededicate ourselves to serving the common good. We are a community. Out individual fates are linked; our futures intertwined; and if we act in that knowledge and that spirit, as the Bible says: 'We can move mountains'" (p. 126).

In her essay "The Roots of War," Ayn Ryan held that the major wars of history were started by the more controlled economics of the time against the freer ones and that capitalism gave mankind the longest period of peace in history, a period in which there were no wars involving the entire civilized world from the end of the Napoleonic wars in 1815 to the outbreak of World War I in 1914, with the exception of the Franco-Prussian War (1870), the Spanish American War (1898), and the American Civil War (1861-1865), which notably occurred in perhaps the liberal economy in the world at the beginning of the industrial revolution.

Traditionally, Hinduism has adopted an ancient Sanskrit phrase, *Vasudha eka Kutumbakam*, which translates as "The world is one family." The essence of this concept is the observation that only base minds see dichotomies and divisions. The more we seek wisdom, the more we become inclusive and free our eternal spirit from worldly or Maya. World peace is hence only achieved through internal means by liberating ourselves from artificial boundaries that separate us all. As with all Dharmic religions (Hinduism, Jainism, Buddhism, and Sikhism), *ahimsa* (avoidance of violence) is a central concept (World Peace, Wikipedia). According to Islamic teachings, the journey to true inner peace and tranquillity involves an absolute faith and obedience through worship of one only God, the source of Ultimate Peace. The knowledge of having a common ancestry derived from Adam and Eve is evoked as a reminder for men and women to suppress the poisonous ideology of racial superiority and to enable communities and nations to live together in this shared world, in peace and harmony.

"The International Day of Peace, sometimes unofficially known as World Peace Day observed annually on 21 November. It is dedicated to peace, and specifically the absence of war and violence, such as might be occasioned by a temporary ceasefire in a combat zone for humanitarian aid access. The day was first celebrated in 1982, and is kept by many nations, political groups, and peoples. In 2013, for the first time, the day was dedicated to peace education, i.e. by the preventive means to reduce war sustainably" (Wikipedia).

"This world feels itself like a man who continues putting off some unpleasant business from day to day, yet knows it must be done, hates to set about it, wishes it over and is continuously haunted with the thought of its necessity" (Thomas Paine, *Common Sense*, p. 56).

We must realize that this is a changing world. It is possible that politicians, or world leaders, might allow a misunderstanding to throw the superpowers into a nuclear war. This of course must be avoided by those in power.

We will never pass this way again. Therefore, let us give our best efforts, with a real desire, that is, to succeed in the search for peace.

Today, we stand at the brink of unprecedented global destruction, global warming, and global violence. This violence pushes us personally and internationally ever closer to the abyss of destruction, but the grace of the Sacred Heart-with all its burning social, economic, and political implications-has the power to convert us into people of Gospel nonviolence, pull back from the brink, and create a new world of peace with justice. If we were to adopt the image of the Sacred Heart (of Jesus) as our image of a nonviolent, peacemaking God, and live not just individually but communally, nationally, and globally according to that nonviolent, radiant love, the world would be disarmed (James Martin, S.J.).

Finally, according to Islamic eschatology, the whole world will be united under the leadership of prophet Isa (Jesus) in his second coming. At that time, love, justice, and peace will be so abundant that the world will be in likeness of paradise.

About the Author

Al Lipoid was born on 1928, of immigrant parents (Austria-Hungary) in the coal-mining town of Dawson. New Mexico. He was a World War II Marine Corps veteran. He attended John Carroll University and the Cleveland Marshall Law School (now part of Cleveland State University) where he was awarded a doctor of law degree. He spent most of his legal career as an assistant county prosecuting attorney in Cuyahoga County, Cleveland, Ohio. For five years, he was the first assistant prosecuting attorney Cuyahoga County, Cleveland, Ohio.

He is the author of the book, *The Permanent Establishment of Peace.*

www.ingramcontent.com/pod-product-compliance
Lightning Source LLC
Chambersburg PA
CBHW052043070526
44584CB00018B/2592